STEPS
TO INDEPENDENT LIVING

THIRD
EDITION

How to Stay Healthy

Nancy Lobb

illustrated by David Strauch

WALCH EDUCATION

Certified Chain of Custody
Promoting Sustainable
Forest Management

www.sfiprogram.org

SGS-SFI/COC-US09/5501

1   2   3   4   5   6   7   8   9   10

ISBN 978-0-8251-6491-0

Copyright © 1986, 1995, 2009
J. Weston Walch, Publisher
40 Walch Drive • Portland, ME 04103

Printed in the United States of America

Contents

© 2009 Walch Education

Part 3: Good Nutrition Is More Than an Apple a Day

Part 4: Fitness for Life

To the Student

Living on your own can be a great experience! You can choose and decorate your own place. You can decide for yourself what and when to eat. You can set your own hours. In short, you are free to make your own choices about your lifestyle.

Along with these freedoms comes responsibility. Living on your own means it's up to you to take care of yourself when you're sick or hurt. You are now the one who must be sure your nutritional, physical, and emotional needs are met. No one will be watching over you to ensure your personal safety. No one will be looking to make sure you make good decisions about alcohol, drugs, and tobacco. It's up to you!

But that's not all! You must make good choices as you choose and set up your home. You must keep your home safe and clean. And you must use your money wisely to meet your needs.

You will have a better experience living on your own if you are prepared to meet your new responsibilities. The six books in the *Steps to Independent Living* series will teach you the skills you need to make it on your own.

In this book, *How to Stay Healthy,* you will learn about:

- the importance of good grooming habits

- how to take care of your eyes, ears, nails, and teeth

- good nutrition for better health

- how to stay physically fit

We hope this information helps prepare you for the day you start living on your own!

© 2009 Walch Education

Self-Test

Find out how good your health habits are. Circle YES or NO for each question.

1. Do you know how to keep your hair looking its best?

   YES   NO

2. Do you know how to prevent and treat pimples and blackheads?

   YES   NO

3. Do you know how to choose a sunscreen that's best for your skin?

   YES   NO

4. Do you know the signs of vision problems?

   YES   NO

5. Do you know the signs of hearing loss?

   YES   NO

6. Do you know how to remove plaque from your teeth?

   YES   NO

7. Do you know how to access the Food Pyramid for your age, weight, and height?

   YES   NO

8. Do you know which types of fat to avoid in your diet?

   YES   NO

9. Do you know how to get more fiber in your diet?

   YES   NO

10. Do you know the best ways to control your weight?

    YES   NO

11. Do you know how to build your endurance?

    YES   NO

12. Do you know how to reduce stress in your life?

    YES   NO

13. Do you know how to get more whole grains in your diet?

    YES   NO

14. Do you know which vegetables have the most nutrition?

    YES   NO

15. Do you know which fats to include in your diet?

    YES   NO

How many YES answers did you have? _____

After you read this book, take the self-test again.

How many YES answers did you have this time? _____

© 2009 Walch Education

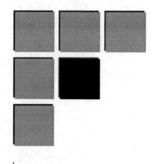

PART 1

Why All the Fuss About Grooming?

Good Grooming Pays Off!

Two students applied for the same part-time job. The first student was neat and well-groomed. The second student had dirty hair and nails, messy clothes, and body odor. The first student got the job. Are you surprised?

It may not seem fair or right. But others do judge you by your appearance. A person who is well-groomed will seem more professional on the job than someone who is careless about his or her appearance. Just as important, well-groomed people will simply feel better about themselves!

What is good grooming? It means taking care of your hair, skin, face, and the rest of your body every day. Good grooming is part of taking good care of yourself.

Keeping Clean

Think about the old cowboy movies. Every Saturday night the cowboys rode into town from the dusty range. They'd head for the bathhouse and plunk down their 25 cents for their weekly bath "whether they needed it or not"!

But body odor isn't really a joking matter. It's unpleasant to be with someone who smells dirty. It can cost a person friends—or even a job.

Luckily, it's easy to get rid of body odor. Take a bath or shower daily. Soap and water will quickly rid your body of dirt and germs. Be sure to rinse off well after bathing to avoid skin irritations. Dry off with a clean towel. Never share towels with another person.

Use perfume, cologne, or aftershave if you like. But use only a little bit! Never use a scent as a substitute for soap and water. And don't forget to put on clean underwear and socks daily, too.

Many people use either a deodorant or antiperspirant daily. What's the difference? A deodorant controls odor. An antiperspirant makes you sweat less. Some products have both a deodorant and an antiperspirant.

Following the steps above every day will help you keep it clean!

© 2009 Walch Education

Lather Up!

You've seen it on TV. "If you want to find true love, you must first use Wonder Mane shampoo." Of course, you know better than that! But everyone does want their hair to look good.

There are hundreds of different shampoos. Does it matter which one you use? How can you choose what's best for your hair? Or are they all the same?

Actually, using the right kind of shampoo will help. Choose a shampoo that's right for your hair type: dry, normal, or oily. If you have dandruff, use a dandruff shampoo. Try several different shampoos that fit your hair type. See which one makes your hair look the best.

© 2009 Walch Education

Wash your hair as often as needed to keep it looking clean. Although you need to wash your body every day, you don't have to wash your hair daily. Before you shampoo, brush your hair. Brushing will loosen dirt and oil and will remove tangles. Then wet your hair with warm (not hot) water.

Follow the directions on the shampoo bottle for the best results. After shampooing, be sure to rinse well. Many people don't rinse long enough to remove all the soap. Soap left in the hair makes it look dull and dirty.

Consider using a conditioner or other hair moisturizer after you shampoo. Conditioners can make hair shiny, smooth, and less messy. If your hair is dry, you need a conditioner or moisturizer each time you shampoo. Otherwise, use it once in a while. If you use conditioner regularly, you may want to try a shampoo that has conditioner already mixed in with the shampoo.

Dry your hair with a clean towel. If you blow-dry your hair, be careful not to use too hot a setting. Don't hold the blow dryer too close to your head. Heat can damage your hair.

Your Crowning Glory

There are two more steps to good-looking hair:

1. brushing or combing your hair correctly
2. getting a good haircut

Brushing Your Hair Correctly

With regular brushing, hair will have fewer mats, tangles, and flyaways.

First, choose the right tool for your hair needs. A very fine-toothed comb removes scalp build-up. A wide-toothed comb or pick is best for combing through hair and will minimize breakage.

A good hairbrush will smooth hair. Make sure the bristles of the brush are not sharp. Natural bristles are better for the hair than nylon bristles. Soft brushes are best for fine or dry hair. Stiffer brushes may be needed for long or thick hair.

Brush or comb your hair several times every day. Take long, smooth strokes from scalp to ends. But don't overdo it. Brushing or combing too hard causes broken hair. Also, brushing wet hair may cause it to break.

Keep your brush, comb, or pick clean. Remove loose hairs. Wash a brush with your shampoo. Air-dry the brush, comb, or pick. Don't use a blow dryer on them.

© 2009 Walch Education

Getting a Good Haircut

Find a good barber or stylist. Work with her or him to decide on a style that looks good on you. Get regular haircuts to help your hair keep its shape. Keep your hair at a length and style that is easy for you to maintain. The barber or stylist can also give you advice on products that will help your hair look its best.

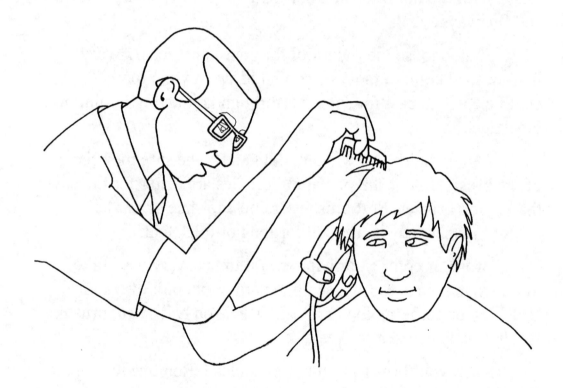

Face the Facts!

You can do two main things to have more attractive skin and to prevent skin problems:

1. keep your skin clean

2. keep healthy by getting good nutrition and enough exercise

Keeping Your Skin Clean

Wash your face with mild soap and warm water morning and night. If your skin is oily, you can wash more often. There are soaps for every type of skin: dry, oily, sensitive, acne-prone, and so on. Deodorant soap is too harsh for your face.

Rinse in warm water, then in cool. Soap left on the skin will make it dry, so wash it all off. If you have dry skin, you may want to use a moisturizing cream or lotion. But if your skin is oily, avoid oily creams or lotions.

Many teenagers have trouble with pimples or blackheads. To prevent and treat acne, follow the steps above. Here are a few more steps:

- Medicated soaps, cleaners, and ointments for acne can help.

- Keep your hair clean and off your face.

- Don't squeeze or pick pimples. That could spread the infection or scar your face.

- If you have severe acne, see a skin doctor for advice. New medicines may help you.

© 2009 Walch Education

Healthy Skin Begins Within

Your skin is like a mirror reflecting your inner health. To have healthy skin, eat a well-balanced diet. Avoid greasy foods. Drink a lot of water every day. Exercise regularly. Get plenty of rest. Do these things, and your skin will look its best.

© 2009 Walch Education

Be Smart in the Sun

Many people like to bask in the sun, hoping to get a suntan. All too often, they end up with too much sun, resulting in a sunburn. Constant tanning and/or burning will cause skin to become wrinkled, dry, and old before its time.

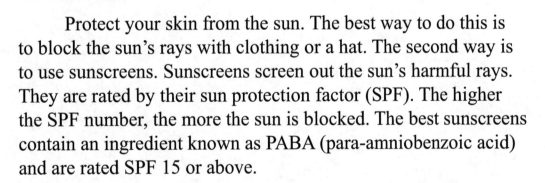

Sun damage is also the leading cause of skin cancer. More than 1 million Americans get skin cancer every year. No matter if your skin tone is fair, medium, dark, or olive, everyone needs protection from sunburn.

Protect your skin from the sun. The best way to do this is to block the sun's rays with clothing or a hat. The second way is to use sunscreens. Sunscreens screen out the sun's harmful rays. They are rated by their sun protection factor (SPF). The higher the SPF number, the more the sun is blocked. The best sunscreens contain an ingredient known as PABA (para-amniobenzoic acid) and are rated SPF 15 or above.

It's important to protect your skin every day, no matter what time of day or what season. Stay out of the sun when it is directly overhead, between 10 A.M. and 2 P.M. Remember that you may get burned on cloudy days and not even know it is happening. Also, don't use tanning beds or sun lamps.

Be extra careful whenever you are near water, sand, or snow. These reflect the sun's rays, increasing your chance of sunburn. If your skin gets wet or if you go swimming, you will wash off the sunscreen. Then you'll need to put on more.

© 2009 Walch Education

Check your skin every month or two. Know your moles, freckles, and beauty marks. That way you'll be aware of any changes in their size, texture, or color. Also, check for sores that don't heal. If you notice an area on your skin that looks unusual, get a doctor to check it out.

If you do get burned, stay out of the sun. Sunburn ointments containing PABA may relieve pain. Taking a cool bath or shower may help. Take aspirin or aspirin substitutes for pain. Drink plenty of fluids. If you get a severe sunburn, see a doctor.

© 2009 Walch Education

Check Yourself

1. Name three ways to get rid of body odor.

   a.

   b.

   c.

2. What is good grooming?

3. What is the difference between antiperspirant and deodorant?

4. Name two benefits of using conditioner on your hair.

   a.

   b.

Continued ➤

© 2009 Walch Education   www.walch.com

5. List three tips for controlling acne.

    a.

    b.

    c.

6. List three ways your diet can help you have healthy skin.

    a.

    b.

    c.

7. Explain how to choose a good sunscreen.

8. Tell what to do in case of a mild sunburn.

Continued ▶

9. Explain the importance of checking the appearance of your freckles, moles, and beauty marks.

10. Explain how to choose a shampoo that will help your hair looks its best.

11. Explain how to brush your hair correctly.

12. Describe the correct way to wash your face.

© 2009 Walch Education

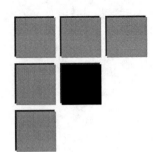

Part 2

Taking Care of
Your Body

The Eyes Have It

How much are your eyes worth to you? No one would want to be without them! Here's how to take good care of your eyes.

1. When you read a book or do close-up work such as writing or drawing, use good light. Light from behind is best. Hold a book at least 12 inches away from your eyes. If you are doing a lot of close work, rest your eyes often to prevent eyestrain.

2. Make sure your computer is set up in a way that will protect your eyes. The light in the room should be low and without glare. Your screen should be approximately 20–26 inches away from you, and slightly below eye level. Take breaks every 10 minutes. Look away from the screen to a distant point so your eyes can adjust and relax.

3. When you watch television, sit at least 10 feet away.

4. Never look directly into the sun. This could cause damage to your eyes.

5. Wear protective goggles if you work with sharp tools or chemicals. If you get a chemical in your eyes, read the label to find out what to do.

6. If you get something in your eye, don't rub it. Rinsing your eye with warm water may help. If something is stuck in your eye, go to a doctor right away.

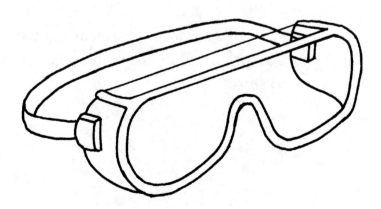

© 2009 Walch Education   www.walch.com

7. Have an eye exam once a year. An eye exam can let you know if you have vision problems or an eye disease. You should have an eye exam if you have any of these signs:

   - trouble seeing clearly (blurry vision either far away or close up)

   - pain in the eyes

   - a lot of headaches or eyestrain

   - double vision

   - halos around lights

   Where should you go for eye care?

   - An ophthalmologist is a medical doctor who tests vision and writes prescriptions for glasses or contact lenses. This doctor can also treat eye diseases and do surgery.

   - Optometrists are trained to test vision and write prescriptions for glasses or contact lenses. Optometrists are not medical doctors.

   - Opticians are technicians who fill the prescription from an ophthalmologist or optometrist. They fit and sell glasses. Some opticians can also fit contact lenses.

   If you need glasses or contact lenses, shop around for the best price and quality. There can be a big difference from store to store.

© 2009 Walch Education

Ear Care

Keep your ears clean for better hearing. Remove earwax in your outer ear (the part of the ear you can see) with a washcloth or cotton swab. Be careful to use the swab only on the outer ear. Otherwise, you could push the earwax back down the ear canal.

Sometimes the ear canal gets clogged up with too much wax. If this happens, a doctor will need to remove the wax.

Never push anything down the ear canal. You could damage your eardrum. Or you could start an infection in your ear. If something becomes stuck in your ear canal, a doctor should remove it.

See a doctor if you have an earache. You could have an ear infection. You may need medicine to take care of the problem.

Be kind to your ears. If you work around loud noise, wear earphones or earplugs. Listening to very loud music for long periods of time can cause hearing loss.

How would you know if you have a hearing loss? If you notice any of these signs, take a hearing test:

- You often have to ask people to repeat what they've said.

- You have to strain to hear.

- You hear ringing or buzzing in your ears.

- You often miss what's said to you.

- You can hear better on the phone than in person.

© 2009 Walch Education

Care of the Nails

Clean, attractive nails are an important part of good grooming. Here's how to keep your nails looking their best:

1. Clean well under each nail. Use soap, water, and a nailbrush if needed.

2. When you dry your hands, gently push back each cuticle with a towel. The cuticle is the strip of hardened skin around the base of the nail. DO NOT clip your cuticles.

3. If you have hangnails, do not pull them off. Cut them with fine scissors.

4. Use clippers to trim your fingernails to an attractive length. Cut them straight across and a little rounded at the corners.

5. Use an emery board to shape and smooth the nails.

6. If you use nail polish, keep it looking fresh. Redo polish as soon as it becomes chipped.

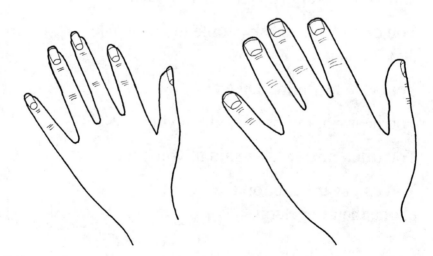

© 2009 Walch Education

A Foot to Stand On

If you take good care of your feet, they won't let you down! Here's how.

Care of Toenails

It's easier to cut your toenails after a bath or shower, when the nails are softer. Wash your feet in warm, soapy water. Push back cuticles with a towel as you dry your feet.

Clip your toenails straight across. DO NOT round the edges. DO NOT clip the nails too short. Short nail edges can grow into the skin, causing a painful ingrown nail. Smooth any rough edges with an emery board.

Keep Those Feet Smelling Sweet!

The best way to prevent foot odor is to wash your feet with soap and water daily, or more often if needed. The socks you wear can make a difference, too. All-cotton socks help prevent foot odor. Nylon socks may make foot odor worse. Be sure to change your socks every day. It can also help to have more than one pair of shoes and alternate wearing them.

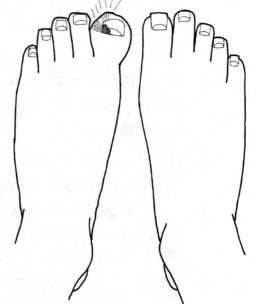

If you try all of these ideas and still have a problem, try putting a bit of talcum powder or baking powder in your shoes.

© 2009 Walch Education

Your Pearly Whites

Keeping your teeth clean helps your teeth and gums stay healthy. It's good for your breath, too.

Brushing and flossing your teeth removes plaque. Plaque causes tooth decay and bad breath. Brush at least twice a day, after breakfast and dinner. Floss your teeth daily.

Here's how to take the best care of your teeth:

1. Use a toothbrush with soft bristles. Choose a size and shape of brush that lets you reach all areas easily. Replace your toothbrush every three or four months. A worn brush won't do a good job cleaning your teeth. Use fluoride toothpaste to make your teeth stronger and to prevent decay.

2. Brush all sides of each tooth, especially the part near the gums. Take your time and do a good job.

3. Every night before bed, clean between your teeth with floss.

4. Using a fluoride mouth rinse can also help prevent decay. Look for the American Dental Association (ADA) seal on the bottle to be sure that the rinse will be effective in preventing cavities.

5. Sugar is the leading cause of tooth decay. So, eat a balanced diet that is low in sugar. Brush your teeth after you eat something sweet.

6. Have a dental checkup every six months. If the cost is a problem, check with a dental school. Or there may be a low-cost dental clinic near you.

Personal Care Checklist

Take a good look at yourself right now. Are you well-groomed? Or do you think your grooming needs improvement?

Mark an X under YES or NO for each item.

		YES	NO
1.	I took a bath or shower in the last 24 hours.	___	___
2.	I used deodorant today.	___	___
3.	My hair is neat, clean, and trimmed.	___	___
4.	My face and hands are clean.	___	___
5.	My ears are clean and free of excess wax.	___	___
6.	My toenails are correctly clipped.	___	___
7.	My fingernails are clean and well shaped.	___	___
8.	I brushed and flossed my teeth last night.	___	___
9.	I brushed my teeth this morning.	___	___
10.	My clothes are neat and clean.	___	___
11.	I put on clean underwear and socks today.	___	___
12.	My shoes are clean and/or polished.	___	___
13.	I used little or no cologne/aftershave.	___	___
14.	My makeup (if any) is neat and not overdone.	___	___
15.	My face is clean-shaven, or my beard or moustache is neatly trimmed.	___	___
16.	I like the way I look today.	___	___

If you really wanted to impress someone today, what changes would you need to make in your grooming?

© 2009 Walch Education

Check Yourself

1. Name three signs that you should get an eye exam.

    a.

    b.

    c.

2. What kind of lighting is best for reading or close work?

3. Name three signs of possible hearing loss.

    a.

    b.

    c.

4. Which eye professional is a medical doctor?

Continued ➡

5. What should you do if a chemical splashes in your eyes?

6. What is the purpose of a yearly eye exam?

7. How should you clean your ears safely?

8. What should you do if you get an earache?

9. What should you do if your ear canal is clogged with wax?

10. What should you do if you get a hangnail?

Continued ▶

© 2009 Walch Education

11. How should you keep your cuticles attractive?

12. How can you avoid getting ingrown toenails?

13. What kind of socks are best for preventing foot odor?

14. Put an X next to each step you take to care for your teeth.

_____ Use a toothbrush with firm bristles.

_____ Floss weekly.

_____ Avoid touching the gums with your toothbrush.

_____ Eat a diet that is low in sugar.

_____ Have a dental checkup every two years.

_____ Use fluoride toothpaste.

_____ Use fluoride mouth rinse with the ADA seal.

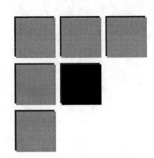

PART 3

Good Nutrition Is
More Than an Apple a Day

The Food Pyramid

Here's a pointed reminder for the way we should choose what we eat: the USDA Food Guide Pyramid. Unlike the pyramids of Egypt, this pyramid is no mystery.

Below is a picture of the food pyramid for an 18-year-old male (170 pounds, 5' 10", and moderate activity level).

| Grains | Vegetables | Fruits | Milk | Meat & Beans |

Each part of the pyramid has a message. Here is what it says:

1. The person climbing the stairs is a reminder that everyone needs to be physically active. Running, walking, swimming, or playing sports are all good ways to stay in shape. We'll talk more about this on pages 62–63.

2. The five wide stripes stand for the five food groups. The food groups are:

- Grains

- Vegetables

- Fruits

- Milk

- Meats and beans

3. A sixth narrow stripe stands for oils and fats. Oils and fats are not a food group. But you need a small amount of healthy oils in your daily diet.

4. The food pyramid can be personalized just for you. Go to <u>www.mypyramid.gov</u>. Enter your age, gender, weight, height, and activity level. You will get a pyramid to meet your needs.

© 2009 Walch Education

The Grains Group

Grains are foods made from wheat, rice, corn, oats, barley, or another cereal grain. Noodles, cereal, tortillas, bread, popcorn, and crackers are all in the grains group.

There are two kinds of grains. Whole grains include the whole-grain kernel. (This includes the bran, germ, and endosperm.) Whole-grain bread, oatmeal, brown rice, and whole cornmeal are examples of whole grains.

Refined grains have been processed. This gives them a finer texture. But processing also removes fiber, iron, and vitamins. Most refined grains are also "enriched." This means that some vitamins have been added back after the grain is processed.

Be sure at least half the grains you eat are whole grains. How can you tell if a grain product is whole grain? Look at the label. The first ingredient listed should say "whole grain." If it says "enriched flour," it is not a whole-grain product.

© 2009 Walch Education

Whole grains:	**Refined grains:**
brown rice	saltine crackers
oatmeal	white enriched bread
popcorn	white noodles
whole-wheat bread	spaghetti
whole-grain cereal	corn flakes
whole-wheat rolls	white hamburger buns
whole-grain cornmeal	white rice

List the grains you ate yesterday. Circle each food that is a whole-grain food. Were half of your grain choices from the whole-grain group?

An 18-year-old female (5'4" and 135 pounds) should have 6 ounces of grains a day. An 18-year-old male (5'10" and 170 pounds) should have 10. Half of these should be whole grains. How did you do?

© 2009 Walch Education

The Vegetable Group

Eat a variety of vegetables daily. Any vegetable or 100% vegetable juice counts! Vegetables may be raw or cooked. They may be frozen, fresh, dried, or canned.

Vegetables are often put into one of five groups. Each group has different types of nutrients. Choose vegetables that are dark green or orange for the most nutrition.

Here are a few examples from each group:

1. **Dark green vegetables**

   Broccoli, spinach, turnip greens, dark green leaf lettuce

2. **Orange vegetables**

   Carrots, sweet potatoes, pumpkin, and orange squashes (butternut, acorn, and hubbard)

3. **Starchy vegetables**

   White potatoes, corn, green peas, lima beans

4. **Dry beans and peas**

   Black beans, kidney beans, black-eyed peas, lentils, or other dried peas or beans

5. **Other vegetables**

   Tomatoes, celery, cabbage, cauliflower, onions, beets, zucchini

© 2009 Walch Education

An 18-year-old female (5'4" and 135 pounds) should have 3 cups of vegetables a day. An 18-year-old male (5'10" and 170 pounds) should have 4.

List the vegetables you ate yesterday.

How did you do?

© 2009 Walch Education

The Fruit Group

Eat plenty of fruit every day. Any fruit or 100% fruit juice counts! Fresh fruit is great. Canned, frozen, or dried fruits are good, too.

Be careful about fruit juices. Many juice products have lots of sugar added. Many are mostly sugar water with only a small amount of fruit. Check the label. Be sure you are drinking 100% fruit juice.

Here are some examples of fruits:

Apples	Nectarines
Apricots	Oranges
Avocados	Peaches
Bananas	Pears
Berries	Pineapples
Cherries	Raisins
Grapefruit	Orange juice (100%)
Grapes	Apple juice (100%)
Lemons	Grape juice (100%)
Melons	Grapefruit juice (100%)

© 2009 Walch Education

An 18-year-old female (5'4" and 135 pounds) should have 3 cups of fruit a day. An 18-year-old male (5'10" and 170 pounds) should have 4.

List the fruits you ate yesterday.

How did you do?

© 2009 Walch Education   www.walch.com

The Milk Group

The milk group includes all liquid forms of milk. It also includes many foods made from milk. To be part of the milk group, a food must contain calcium.

Some foods made from milk actually have little calcium. Examples are butter, cream cheese, and cream. "Cheese food" is made from vegetable oil. None of these foods are considered servings of the milk group.

Milk and milk products are needed to build strong bones and healthy teeth. Be sure the products you choose say "low fat" or "fat free" on the label. Avoid drinking whole or 2% milk products. These add extra fat and calories to your diet. Drinking skim milk gives you the same amount of calcium with far fewer calories.

Here are some examples of the milk group:

Milk:

All kinds of milk

Flavored milk

Lactose-free milk

Desserts made from milk:

Pudding

Frozen yogurt

Ice milk

Ice cream

Cheese:

Cheddar cheese

Mozzarella cheese

Swiss cheese

Parmesan cheese

Cottage cheese

American cheese

Yogurt: all kinds

© 2009 Walch Education   www.walch.com

Both an 18-year-old female (5'4" and 135 pounds) and an 18-year-old male (5'10" and 170 pounds) should have three servings from the milk group daily. This could be 3 cups of liquid milk, cottage cheese, or yogurt. An ounce and a half of cheese is equal to a cup of milk.

List the milk products you ate yesterday.

How did you do?

The Meat and Beans Group

Meats are a good source of protein. Choose meats that are lean or low fat. Trim all visible fats from meats before cooking. Do the same at the table. Eat lean chicken, beef, pork, turkey, or fish.

Dry beans and peas are a good source of protein, too. There are many different kinds. Some examples are black beans, pinto beans, and black-eyed peas.

Nuts are a good source of protein. Try peanuts, almonds, or other nuts.

Here are some examples of foods in the meat group:

Meats:

Beef

Ham

Lamb

Pork

Ground meats

Game

Fish:

Catfish

Cod

Flounder

Salmon

Trout

Tuna

Shellfish:

Clams

Crab

Lobster

Shrimp

Poultry:

Chicken

Turkey

Duck

© 2009 Walch Education

Nuts and Seeds:	**Dry beans and peas:**
Almonds	Black beans
Cashews	Black-eyed peas
Peanuts/peanut butter	Kidney beans
Pecans	Lentils
Sunflower seeds	Lima beans
Walnuts	Navy beans
	Pinto beans, split peas
Eggs	Tofu

An 18-year-old female (5'4" and 135 pounds) should have 6 one-ounce equivalents from the meat group daily. An 18-year-old male (5'10" and 170 pounds) should have 7. List the foods you ate yesterday from the meat and beans group.

How did you do?

(A one-ounce equivalent is one of the following: an ounce of meat, chicken, or fish; one egg; one tablespoon of peanut butter; half an ounce of nuts; or one-quarter cup of cooked dry beans. Four ounces of meat can fit on the palm of your hand.)

Oils and Fats

Oils and fats are not a food group. You need only a tiny amount of these in your diet. However, most Americans eat far more fat than they need! Eating too much fat can increase your risk of heart disease, diabetes, some types of cancer, and high blood pressure. There are four main groups of fats and oils.

The first two kinds of fat are saturated fats and trans fats. These fats should be very limited in the diet. They can raise your cholesterol. They can cause fatty build-up on the inside of your arteries. That can lead to heart disease.

The American Heart Association says you should have no more than 7% of your daily calories from saturated fats. Limit trans fats to one gram a day. How can you do this? Trim all fat you can see off meat. Read labels on products you buy. Choose those with little saturated fat and no trans fat.

1. Saturated fats come from animal products. Examples are meat fat, whole milk, cream, whole-milk cheeses, butter, egg yolks, and lard. Some plant oils are saturated fats. These include palm oil, palm kernel oil, coconut oil, and cocoa butter.

2. Trans fats are found in partially hydrogenated vegetable oils. They are often found in cookies, crackers, cakes, French fries, doughnuts, and other foods. Read product labels to see if they contain trans fats.

© 2009 Walch Education

The second two kinds of fats are polyunsaturated and monounsaturated fats. These unsaturated fats can help keep blood cholesterol down. They can reduce cholesterol deposits in the arteries. Both polyunsaturated fats and monounsaturated fats are liquid at room temperature. Unsaturated fats should still be used in moderation. They are high in calories.

3. Monounsaturated fats are found in olive oil, canola oil, peanut oil, and avocados.

4. Polyunsaturated fats are found in safflower oil, sesame oil, soybean oil, corn oil, sunflower oil, and nuts and seeds.

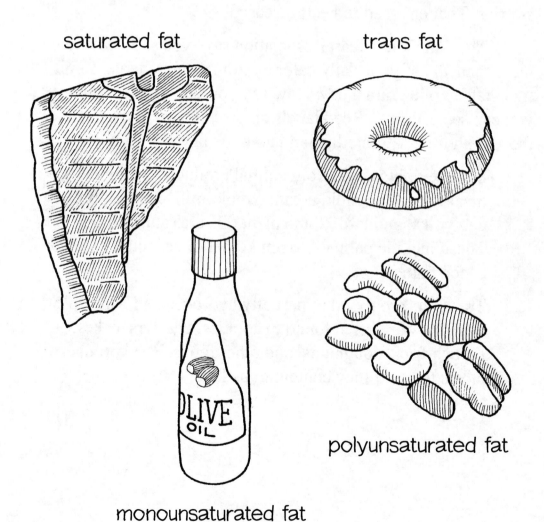

saturated fat

trans fat

polyunsaturated fat

monounsaturated fat

Nutritious Nutrients

There are six types of nutrients in food. If you eat enough foods from the USDA Food Guide Pyramid and drink plenty of water every day, you should get enough of each nutrient that your body needs.

1. **Your body needs protein.** Proteins help your body's cells grow and repair themselves. Proteins can also supply some energy. Proteins are found in meat, eggs, cheese, milk, dried beans and peas, grains, and nuts.

2. **Your body needs carbohydrates.** Carbohydrates are the body's main source of energy. They are found in breads, cereals, vegetables, and fruits. They are also found in sugars.

3. **Your body needs a very small amount of fats.** Fats are a source of energy. But if you eat too much fat, you may gain body fat. That's because your body makes fat to store the energy from the extra calories you eat. Fatty foods have a lot of extra calories. Fats are found in meats, dairy foods, and oils. They are also present in many other foods.

4. **Your body needs vitamins.** Vitamins regulate many body processes. If you eat a balanced diet, you should get all the vitamins you need. If not, you may need to take vitamin pills. Ask your doctor if you need extra vitamins.

5. **Your body needs minerals.** Minerals such as calcium, iron, fluoride, and phosphorus build bones and teeth and regulate body processes.

6. **Your body needs water.** Water carries out waste, carries food to the cells, and keeps your body at the correct temperature. Drink plenty of water every day.

You Are What You Eat

Your body is made from the food you eat. To have a healthy body, a healthy diet is a must! Scientists have proven that eating a poor diet is a serious health risk. Here are four things to keep in mind for a better diet and better health.

Eat Less Fat

A small amount of fat is necessary in the diet for the body to function properly. But most Americans eat far more fat than they need! Eating too much fat can increase your risk of heart disease, diabetes, some types of cancer, and high blood pressure.

Make sure the fats and oils you eat are good ones. (See pages 43–44.) Get your fats from fish, nuts, and liquid oils such as olive oil, canola oil, corn oil, or soybean oil.

Eat Less Salt

The body needs small amounts of salt to control its water balance and maintain heart rhythm. Most of us eat far more salt than necessary. Too much salt has been linked to high blood pressure. It's best not to eat too much salt with your food!

© 2009 Walch Education

Eat Less Sugar

Sugar is a source of energy. But most of our diets contain way too much sugar. If you eat too much sugar, some is stored as fat. Being overweight leads to heart disease and high blood pressure. It also increases the risk of developing diabetes.

The other problem caused by sugar is tooth decay. Bacteria living in the mouth eat the sugar. They then release an acid that makes holes in teeth.

Read the label to see how much sugar is in a food. But watch out! Not all sugars are labeled as "sugar" on the label. Other names for sugar are: corn syrup, high-fructose corn syrup, fruit juice concentrate, maltose, dextrose, sucrose, honey, and maple syrup.

Eat More Fiber

Fiber comes from plants. It makes the waste in the intestines soft so the waste can be moved along easily. This helps keep the intestines free of disease.

Fiber is found in foods made from whole grains. It is also found in vegetables, cereals, fruits, and brans. Foods made from white flour often contain little fiber. These foods are not as good for you as foods made from whole grains.

© 2009 Walch Education

Read the Label for Better Nutrition

Reading food labels can help you choose foods that are good for you. Each label has six main parts. We will look at each part and see what you can learn from it.

1. Serving information
2. Calorie information
3. Nutrients to limit (fat, cholesterol, sodium)
4. Nutrients to get (fiber, vitamins, minerals)
5. Footnote
6. Ingredients

Nutrition Facts

Serving Size 1/2 Pizza (153g)
Servings Per Container 2

Amount Per Serving	1/2 pizza		1 pizza	
Calories	420		840	
Calories from Fat	170		350	
		% DV*		**% DV***
Total Fat	19g	**29%**	39g	**60%**
Saturated Fat	8g	**40%**	15g	**75%**
Trans Fat	1.5g		3g	
Cholesterol	25mg	**8%**	55mg	**18%**
Sodium	910mg	**38%**	1810mg	**75%**
Total Carbohydrate	44g	**15%**	89g	**30%**
Dietary Fiber	4g	**16%**	7g	**28%**
Sugars	7g		14g	
Protein	17g		35g	
Vitamin A		10%		20%
Vitamin C		0%		2%
Calcium		15%		30%
Iron		10%		20%

*Percent Daily Values (DV) are based on a 2,000 calorie diet. Your daily values may be higher or lower depending on your calorie needs:

	Calories:	2,000	2,500
Total Fat	Less than	65g	80g
Sat Fat	Less than	20g	25g
Cholest	Less than	300mg	300mg
Sodium	Less than	2,400mg	2,400mg
Total Carb		300g	375g
Fiber		25g	30g

Ingredients: Crust (wheat flour, crust mix [wheat gluten, oat flour, oat fiber, oat syrup solids, barley malt extract, triticale flour, brown rice flour, red wheat flour, rye flour, salt, barley flour, buckwheat flour, sesame seed], water, yeast, ground flaxseed, extra virgin olive oil), cheese blend (mozzarella cheese [pasteurized part-skim cow's milk, cheese cultures, salt, enzymes], white cheddar cheese [pasteurized milk, cheese cultures, salt, enzymes, calcium chloride], yellow cheddar cheese [pasteurized milk, cheese cultures, salt, enzymes, calcium chloride, annatto color], asiago cheese [pasteurized part-skim cow's milk, cheese cultures, salt, microbial rennet]), sauce (water, diced tomatoes in juice [diced tomatoes, tomato juice, salt, calcium chloride, citric acid], tomato paste [tomatoes], sauce mix [cane juice solids, maltodextrin, dehydrated garlic, cornstarch, salt, spices and spice extractives, xanthan gum, citric acid], extra virgin olive oil), diced tomatoes (tomato, calcium chloride), parmesan cheese (pasteurized part-skim milk, cheese culture, salt, enzymes), basil, oregano.

1. **Serving information.** Here you can learn what makes a serving. You also find out how many servings are in a package. One serving of this pizza is only half a pizza. If you eat the whole thing (and you might because it's not very big!), you have eaten two servings!

2. **Calorie information.** Here you find the number of calories in one serving of this pizza. There are 420 calories in one serving. Remember, that means only half of the pizza. If you eat the whole thing, you have eaten 840 calories! Also, you learn that a serving of this pizza has 170 calories from fat. That is almost half of the total number of calories per 420-calorie serving!

3. **Nutrients to limit.** This part of the label lists amounts of fat, cholesterol, and sodium in the food. These are things most of us eat too much of! One serving of this pizza has 19 grams of fat. Of these, 8 grams are saturated fat and 1.5 grams are trans fat. There are 25 mg of cholesterol. There are also 910 mg of sodium (salt).

   It's best to choose foods with very little or no saturated fat, trans fat, or cholesterol. This product is loaded with all three, plus sodium! There are better choices for your meal.

4. **Nutrients to get.** Many people don't get enough fiber, vitamins A and C, calcium, and iron in their diets. This part of the label can help you see how to get more of these important nutrients in your diet. Looking at the pizza label, we see that a serving has 10% of the daily requirement of vitamin A and 0% of vitamin C. It has 15% of the calcium requirement. And it has only 10% of the iron needed. (These percents are based on a 2,000-calorie diet.)

5. **Footnote.** The footnote is the same on every food label. (It is not on every package. If the label is too small, it will be omitted.) The footnote tells you the Percent Daily Value recommended for a 2,000-calorie and a 2,500-calorie diet.

6. **Ingredients.** This part of the label lists all the ingredients in the product. They are listed in order from most to least. For this pizza, wheat flour is listed first.

© 2009 Walch Education

Comparing Labels

Look at the labels from two cartons of yogurt. Then answer the questions below.

Light Yogurt

Original Yogurt

Nutrition Facts

Serving Size 1 container
Servings Per Container 2

Amount Per Serving

Calories 100	Calories from Fat 0

	% Daily Value*
Total Fat 0g	**0%**
Saturated Fat 0g	**0%**
Trans Fat 0g	
Cholesterol less that 5mg	**1%**
Sodium 90g	**4%**
Potassium 260mg	**7%**
Total Carbohydrate 20g	**7%**
Sugars 14g	
Protein 5g	**10%**

Vitamin A 15% • Calcium 20%
Vitamin D 20% • Phosphorus 15%

Not a significant source of dietary fiber,
vitamin C and iron.
*Percent Daily Values are based on a 2,000
calorie diet.

Nutrition Facts

Serving Size 1 container
Servings Per Container 2

Amount Per Serving

Calories 170	Calories from Fat 15

	% Daily Value*
Total Fat 1.5g	**3%**
Saturated Fat 1g	**5%**
Trans Fat 0g	
Cholesterol 10mg	**3%**
Sodium 80g	**3%**
Potassium 260mg	**7%**
Total Carbohydrate 33g	**11%**
Sugars 27g	
Protein 5g	**11%**

Vitamin A 15% • Calcium 20%
Vitamin D 20% • Phosphorus 15%

Not a significant source of dietary fiber,
vitamin C and iron.
*Percent Daily Values are based on a 2,000
calorie diet.

1.   Which yogurt has more calories?

2. Which yogurt has more calories from fat?

3. Which yogurt has more saturated fat?

4. Which yogurt would be a better choice for a low-fat diet?

5. Which yogurt has more sugars?

6. Which yogurt has more protein?

7. Which yogurt has more calcium?

8. Which yogurt would you choose? Explain your answer.

9. Why do you think a person might choose the yogurt you
    did not choose?

© 2009 Walch Education

Watch Those Scales!

Staying at a healthy weight is important for good health. If you are overweight, you have a higher risk of developing high blood pressure, type 2 diabetes, stroke, and some kinds of cancer.

The key to staying at a healthy weight is simple. You must eat the same number of calories as your body uses. If you eat more calories than your body can use, you'll gain weight. If you eat fewer calories than your body needs, you'll lose weight. It sounds easy. But for many people, weight control is easier said than done.

Here are some basic steps for maintaining a healthy weight:

1. Study the food pyramid. Know what kinds of foods your body needs each day.

2. Pay attention to how much you eat. Learn how much of a food is in one serving.

3. Choose foods that are "nutrient-dense." These types of foods have a lot of nutrients but little sugar or fat to add unneeded calories. Avoid junk foods.

4. Weigh yourself at least once a week. If you see your weight creeping up, get it under control fast.

5. Eat slowly at meals. This will help you feel as if you've had more food.

6. Exercise helps burn the calories you eat. It can also help cut your appetite. Exercise at least 30 minutes a day.

7. Keep low-calorie nutritious foods on hand for snacks. Don't buy junk foods. These have a lot of empty calories.

Check Yourself

1. Name the six parts of the food pyramid.

   a.

   b.

   c.

   d.

   e.

   f.

2. What is the purpose of showing the person jogging up the side of the food pyramid?

3. Why are whole grains more nutritious than refined products?

Continued

© 2009 Walch Education

4. Give three examples of whole-grain foods.

    a.

    b.

    c.

5. Which two colors of vegetables pack the most nutrition?

6. Why should you read the label when choosing a fruit drink?

7. Name two kinds of fats to avoid in your diet.

    a.

    b.

8. Give one other name for sugar found on food labels.

Continued ▶

© 2009 Walch Education   www.walch.com

9. What is the key to staying at a healthy weight?

10. Name two problems that could come from eating too much saturated or trans fat.

    a.

    b.

11. Name two ways to cut down on total fat in your diet.

    a.

    b.

12. Name two fats or oils that are beneficial to your health in small amounts.

    a.

    b.

Continued

13. List some foods that are rich in fiber.

14. How can you tell how much fat is in a food before you buy it?

15. How would you know which ingredient is contained in the largest amount in a food?

© 2009 Walch Education

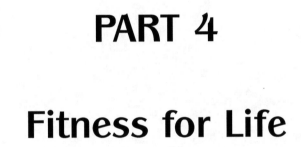

PART 4

Fitness for Life

Are You Physically Fit?

What is being fit? Being fit is feeling good! A fit body can lead to a fit mind as well. You will feel more alert and have more energy if you're fit. Exercise can help you work off stress and take your mind off your problems. Exercise can help you have healthy weight, too.

Being fit gets under your skin! Exercise cuts down the risk of heart disease. It makes the heart muscles stronger. It helps your internal organs work better and stay healthy. All your body systems will work better if you are strong and fit.

There are three parts to physical fitness: endurance, strength, and flexibility.

Endurance

Are you out of breath after you run up the stairs? If so, you need to work on your endurance. Endurance means you can exercise without getting tired quickly. Building your endurance helps you have a strong heart and healthy lungs.

Endurance exercises are activities that increase your heart and breathing rates. If you are out of shape, build up your endurance a little at a time. Start small. You may need to start with 5 or 10 minutes of activity at a time. Add a little more over time. Build up to at least 30 minutes of endurance exercise most days of the week.

© 2009 Walch Education

Strength

Do your arms get tired carrying in the groceries? If so, you need to work on muscle strength. Most strength exercises involve pushing or lifting weights. You can buy small hand and ankle weights. Or you can use cans as weights.

Experts recommend starting with small one- or two-pound weights. Then add more. Work each muscle group at least twice a week. Don't work on the same muscle group two days in a row.

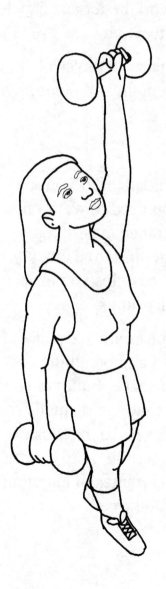

© 2009 Walch Education

Flexibility

If you're flexible, your body bends easily. Being flexible lets you move more gracefully. More important, flexibility cuts down your risk of injury when you're exercising or playing sports.

Stretching exercises can improve your flexibility. They do not help your endurance or strength. Do stretching exercises before and after your endurance and strength exercises.

Before you exercise, warm up. Start slowly by doing some simple stretching exercises. When you finish your exercise period, cool down by doing some of the same stretching exercises. This way you are much less likely to strain your muscles.

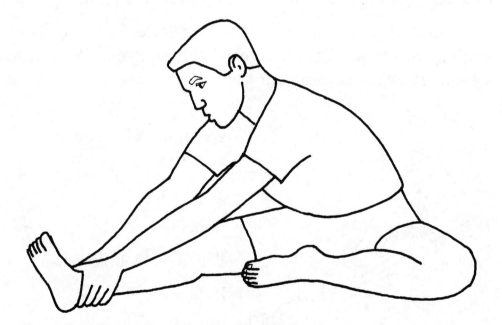

Don't overdo it! If you're not used to exercising, start slowly. Build up a little at a time. If you're very sore, you've overdone it.

© 2009 Walch Education

Physical Activity

Experts recommend at least 30 to 60 minutes of moderate or vigorous physical activity a day. What does that mean?

Any kind of movement is physical activity. Cleaning your home, walking, working in the garden, or playing basketball are all forms of physical activity. So are walking to the mailbox, changing classes at school, or grocery shopping. But not all these could be called "moderate" or "vigorous" activity. That's because they don't raise your heart rate.

So, what's the best way to exercise? Some people like team sports. Others enjoy activities such as walking, skating, or bike riding. Choose something you enjoy doing. Vary your activity from day to day if you want to. But try to stick with it.

Almost anyone can, and should, exercise. But if you have health problems or are overweight, check with your doctor before beginning an exercise program.

Examples of moderate activity:

Yard work

Dancing

Walking at a brisk pace

Hiking

Riding a bicycle (less than 10 mph)

Weight training (a light workout)

© 2009 Walch Education

Doubles tennis

Riding a stationary bicycle

Scrubbing the floor

Volleyball

Yoga

Examples of vigorous activity:

Running or jogging

Shoveling snow

Digging holes

Singles tennis

Swimming laps

Aerobics

Chopping wood

Weight lifting

Playing basketball

Riding a bicycle
(over 10 mph or up
a steep hill)

© 2009 Walch Education

List the moderate or vigorous exercise you've had this past week.

Day	Type of exercise	Amount of time
Sunday		
Monday		
Tuesday		
Wednesday		
Thursday		
Friday		
Saturday		

How did you do?

Did you get 30 to 60 minutes of moderate or vigorous exercise daily?

If not, what could you do to improve?

© 2009 Walch Education

Carrying Your Own Weight

Your posture (the way you hold your body) plays a big part in your appearance. By standing and sitting correctly, you instantly look slimmer. You'll feel more alert when you stand or sit tall. Good posture makes you look and feel better.

Check your standing posture. Stand up with your back pressed against a wall. Place your feet about three inches away from the wall. If you have good posture, your head, shoulders, and buttocks all touch the wall. The small of your back should be about an inch from the wall.

Check your sitting posture. Sit in your chair as you normally do. If you have good sitting posture, your back is flat against the chair back. Your feet are flat on the floor. Slumping in your seat is an example of poor posture. You may have your legs crossed at the ankles or the knees.

Good posture habits are learned. If you decide your posture could be better, improve by practicing and thinking about it. Regular exercise will help your posture, too. Exercising helps you hold your body better.

How Does Your Posture Rate?

1. Are you satisfied with your standing posture? If not, describe what you need to do to improve.

2. Are you satisfied with your sitting posture? If not, describe what you need to do to improve.

© 2009 Walch Education

At Ease!

Most people spend about one-third of their lives sleeping. Sleep is the way the body protects itself from working too hard.

What makes you tired (fatigued)? There are several kinds of fatigue: physical, mental, illness-related, and stress-related.

Physical Fatigue

If you've been exercising hard, you feel physical fatigue. Your muscles are tired. Now you need to do something less active so your muscles can rest. Fresh air can help, too. It gives you more oxygen for your muscles.

Mental Fatigue

If you've been studying for several hours, your mind needs a rest. The best way to feel better is to get some exercise. This will rest your mind and also get the blood circulating.

© 2009 Walch Education   www.walch.com

Illness-Related Fatigue

Many illnesses cause fatigue. This is your signal to get extra rest so your body can heal itself. If you're always tired and don't know why, see a doctor for a checkup to rule out any medical problem.

Stress-Related Fatigue

Stress is anything in your life that makes you feel upset or worried. If you are under stress, you may feel very tired. Many people who don't know how to escape stress end up with stomach trouble, headaches, backaches, or insomnia (they can't sleep well).

Some people may try to reduce stress by drinking alcohol, taking drugs, smoking, or overeating. These habits are harmful to the body. They don't reduce stress, either.

© 2009 Walch Education

Follow these steps to reduce the effects of stress-related fatigue in your life:

1. Exercise regularly. You can blow off a lot of steam in a good workout.

2. Get enough sleep every night.

3. Eat a healthy diet. Drink plenty of water.

4. Keep your work schedule reasonable. Take some time for yourself every day.

5. Learn ways to relax. Prayer, meditation, or yoga might help.

6. Avoid using tobacco, alcohol, or drugs.

7. If you can, change what is causing you stress.

Check Yourself

1. Name five benefits of being physically fit.

    a.

    b.

    c.

    d.

    e.

2. Give three examples of moderate physical activity.

    a.

    b.

    c.

Continued ➤

© 2009 Walch Education

3. Give three examples of vigorous physical activity.

    a.

    b.

    c.

4. What is endurance? How does it help your body?

5. How can you build up your endurance?

6. What is flexibility? Why is it important to you?

7. What is the best way to improve your posture?

Continued

8. How can you avoid muscle strain when exercising?

9. What will give you relief from physical fatigue?

10. What is the best way to find relief from mental fatigue?

11. Name two ways to reduce stress.

    a.

    b.

12. What should you do if you're always tired and don't know why?

© 2009 Walch Education

Words to Know

acne	a skin condition that causes many pimples and blackheads
antiperspirant	a product for controlling sweat
calorie	a unit of energy supplied by food
carbohydrate	a nutrient, such as starch or sugar, that provides fuel for the body
cholesterol	a soft, waxy substance in your blood and cells; high levels of it increase your risk of heart disease
conditioner	a product for making hair manageable
cuticle	a strip of hardened skin around the base of the nail
dandruff	flakes of dead skin on the scalp
dental	a term that refers to teeth and tooth care
deodorant	a product for controlling body odor
ear canal	the canal leading from the outer to the middle ear
emery board	an item used for filing the nails
endurance	the ability to exercise without getting tired quickly
enriched flour	refined grains with some vitamins and iron added back in
fatigue	a feeling of being tired
fiber	indigestible part of plant food that helps move waste out of the body
flexibility	the ability of the body to bend easily
fluoride	a chemical that helps prevent tooth decay
Food Guide Pyramid	the USDA's guide to daily food choices for a healthy diet

© 2009 Walch Education

footnote	a part of many food labels; it gives Percent Daily Value for a 2,000- and a 2,500-calorie diet
grooming	taking care of skin, hair, face, and body to be clean and neat
hangnail	a small piece of skin hanging by one end at the side or base of the nail
ingredient	one of the substances in a food product
ingrown nail	a nail growing back into the skin
insomnia	difficulty sleeping
kernel	a grain or seed such as that of wheat or corn
mental fatigue	a feeling of being tired from using the brain
mineral	a nutrient needed in small amounts for health and growth (examples: iron, calcium)
moderate physical activity	activity that raises the heart rate, such as brisk walking
monounsaturated fat	a type of fat that is liquid at room temperature and helps lower blood cholesterol (found in olive oil, canola oil, peanut oil, avocados)
nutrients	nourishing parts of foods: protein, carbohydrates, vitamins, minerals, fats, and water
nutrition	food, nourishment; the process by which the body takes in and uses nutrients
odor	a smell
ophthalmologist	a medical doctor who tests vision, prescribes glasses and contact lenses, does eye surgery, and treats eye diseases
optician	a technician who fits glasses and sometimes contact lenses using a prescription from the optometrist or ophthalmologist

© 2009 Walch Education

optometrist	a person (not a medical doctor) who tests vision and prescribes glasses and contact lenses
PABA	a substance that blocks ultraviolet rays (para-aminobenzoic acid)
physical fatigue	a feeling of being tired after exercise
plaque	a substance that causes tooth decay and bad breath
polyunsaturated fat	a type of fat that is liquid at room temperature and helps lower blood cholesterol (found in safflower, sesame, soy, corn, and sunflower oils and also in nuts and seeds)
posture	how you hold your body to sit, stand, or walk
protein	a nutrient used by the body to grow and repair itself
refined grain	a grain that has been processed, with some nutrients removed
saturated fat	a fat likely to cause heart disease, usually from animal products
stress	tension, strain, or upset
sun protection factor (SPF)	a number that tells how much of the sun's rays a sunscreen blocks
sunscreen	a product for protecting skin from the sun
trans fat	a bad kind of fat that lowers good cholesterol and raises bad cholesterol; comes from hydrogenated shortening
vigorous physical activity	activity that raises the heart rate, such as jogging, swimming laps, or running
vitamins	nutrients needed in small amounts to regulate body functions (examples: vitamin A, vitamin C)
whole grain	a grain that includes the whole-grain kernel including the bran, germ, and endosperm

© 2009 Walch Education